The Library of the Nine Planets™

URANUS

Jennifer Viegas

rosen
central™

The Rosen Publishing Group, Inc., New York

Published in 2005 by The Rosen Publishing Group, Inc.
29 East 21st Street, New York, NY 10010

Library of Congress Cataloging-in-Publication Data

Viegas, Jennifer.
Uranus/by Jennifer Viegas.
    p. cm.—(The library of the nine planets)
Summary: Presents scientific discoveries about the size, composition, rotation, orbit, and climate of this outer planet that has fifteen moons. Includes bibliographical references and index.
ISBN 1-4042-0174-2 (lib. bdg.)
Uranus (Planet)—Juvenile literature. [1. Uranus (Planet)]
I. Title. II. Series: Planets (Rosen Publishing Group)
QB681.V54 2004
523.47—dc22
                                                          2003022412

Manufactured in the United States of America

On the cover: A computer enhancement of an image of Uranus taken by *Voyager 2.*

Contents

INTRODUCTION

If jet planes could fly through space, it would take one 318.5 years to reach Uranus (YOOR-uh-nus). The trip would be much longer than any human could survive because Uranus, the seventh planet in the solar system, exists deep in space.

Uranus is the third largest of the nine planets in our solar system. But since it is so far away, Uranus looks like a tiny blue-green golf ball when viewed through a telescope from Earth. What looks like a golf ball, though, is actually a large planet.

Sometimes scientists refer to Uranus as a Jovian planet, or a planet that is one of the group consisting of Uranus, Jupiter, Saturn, and Neptune. "Jovian" describes anything having to do with Jupiter, the solar system's largest planet. And, like Jupiter, the other Jovian planets are composed of gas. Because of this, they are also sometimes called the gas giants.

The four Jovian planets of Jupiter, Saturn, Neptune, and Uranus are the largest in our solar system. They consist primarily of frozen gases and there is no solid land on them. Even if a person could travel by plane to Uranus, the visitor would not be able to set foot on the planet. Like the bubbles in soda, gas is extremely lightweight. Although Uranus and the other gas planets are huge, they are very light for their size.

The gas also blocks the view of Uranus by observers. This has puzzled astronomers and space fans for centuries. Imagine if someone asked you to describe the features of a man standing miles away with a paper bag over his head. It would create a near impossible challenge. Even if you got up close to the person, you would still have to guess what he looked like under the bag. The blue-green gas surrounding Uranus serves as such a covering. It presents an obstacle for anyone trying to study the planet.

A number of theories have been proposed for what lies under Uranus's mysterious veil. Some scientists have speculated that a gigantic ocean encircles the planet. Still others have said countless diamonds may shimmer under the surface because diamonds form from carbon that is subjected to extreme temperature and pressure. Such conditions may exist on Uranus. A few researchers even propose that unknown life-forms may lurk under the veil.

High-tech telescopes, space probes, and other equipment in recent years have led to some remarkable discoveries about Uranus. This equipment helps to either disprove or verify much of the speculation about the seventh planet from the Sun. What has been discovered may surprise you.

One

The History of Uranus

Until the late 1700s, people did not realize the universe was so vast. Only five planets, not including Earth, were known to exist. They were Jupiter, Mars, Mercury, Saturn, and Venus.

From Earth, these five planets appear big and bright enough to view with the naked eye. Today we spend many evenings indoors watching television and movies, but in ancient times, the night sky with its spectacular changing light show captured everyone's attention. Polish astronomer Nicolaus Copernicus paid particular interest to celestial happenings.

Looking to the Stars

Before the publication of Copernicus's book *On the Revolutions of the Heavenly Spheres* in 1543, people thought that Earth was the center of the universe with all planets and stars circling around it. Through observations and mathematical calculations, Copernicus disproved this idea. Copernicus said that the six known planets orbited, or revolved around, the Sun. In doing so, he changed the way we view the universe. Though Copernicus's theory was rejected at first, more individuals eventually began to look toward space for answers to the mysteries of the universe.

In response to this growing interest in space science, the Italian astronomer Galileo Galilei first used the telescope around 1608. Galileo's telescope probably had about

If it weren't for William Herschel, we might never have known Uranus existed. An avid astronomer, Herschel is shown here with his sister, Caroline Lucretia Herschel, who was also an astronomer. They are making observations that would lead to the discovery of Uranus in 1781. With this telescope, they also discovered two satellites of Uranus (Titania and Oberon) and two of Saturn (Mimas and Enceladus).

as much power as inexpensive binoculars do today. For its time, however, the telescope was a scientific wonder. Galileo and his colleagues used the device to find the Milky Way and some of Jupiter's moons. Amateur and professional astronomers who learned about Galileo's invention attempted to create telescopes of their own.

German-born musician William Herschel, born in 1738, developed a passion for telescopes and astronomy while attempting to improve his musical studies. Chords, harmony, and other aspects of music involve mathematical principles. Herschel's interest in these principles led him to study both math and space. Gradually, his studies in astronomy overtook his musical interests. He devoted greater time and effort toward becoming a scientist and an astronomer.

Inspired by Galileo, Herschel wanted to make the best telescope in the world. In order to do this, an enormous piece of glass would have to be made using techniques not yet fully mastered in the eighteenth century. To create the lens that he was looking for, Herschel designed a telescope that would reflect light. This reflecting telescope was able to work with a smaller mirror, using much less glass while still being effective. The reflecting telescope improved clarity and enabled Herschel to scan the skies with greater precision.

The World's Largest Telescope

After his discovery of Uranus, Herschel became a celebrity, but fame did not slow him down. He used royal grants to build what was then the world's largest telescope, a 40-foot-long (12-meter-long) contraption with a 48-inch (122-centimeter) mirror. With the help of his sister Caroline, who also became a famous astronomer, Herschel would spend evenings climbing the huge telescope's 50-foot (15 m) scaffolding in order to get a better look at Uranus and the other stars and planets. Until his death in 1822, Herschel retained his curiosity about the newly named, yet still mysterious, planet.

Herschel began a series of sky survey projects. He took note of every star, comet, and planet he could see. Other astronomers and scientists praised his first survey, so Herschel began a second sky survey in 1781.

Herschel found new stars and comets. On Tuesday, March 13, 1781, he saw an unusual small disk in the evening sky. Herschel suspected it was a comet, which has a "tail" made of ice, gas, and dust when it travels near the Sun. But this was no ordinary comet, Herschel wrote in a published announcement. The object had no tail and did not look fuzzy like other comets did.

A New Planet

After reading Herschel's announcement, astronomers began to turn their telescopes toward this most unusual "comet." Nevil Maskelyne, the English astronomer to the royal court, was the first to suspect that the bizarre comet may not be a comet at all, but a new planet! Astronomy experts from Russia to Europe used observations and math to calculate the object's orbit.

Astronomers also analyzed old sky maps for possible earlier references to the mysterious object. They found a prior notation dating to 1690. During that year, an Englishman named John Flamsteed documented the object, but he had no idea what it was. As a result, the scientific community did not pay much attention to Flamsteed's find. Herschel pursued the matter more after his own sighting. Within half a year after Herschel's initial discovery, almost all of the experts agreed that the musician turned astronomer had found a new planet.

This illustration shows William Herschel's reflecting telescope. At the time, this forty-foot telescope was the largest in the world. Unlike other reflecting telescopes, the eyepiece was at the open end of the tube. This required the astronomer to climb the scaffolding to take a look. One astronomer broke his arm while doing this.

This fresco, designed by architect Karl Friedrich Schinkel (1781–1841), shows the god Uranus. The fresco is in the vestibule of the Old Museum in Berlin, Germany.

What to Call It?

If, like Herschel, you discovered a planet, what would you name it? Would you name it after yourself or someone you admire? Or would you use a more conventional name in keeping with the names of the other planets? Herschel found himself asking these questions in the fall of 1781 as astronomers urged him to name the new planet.

Herschel wanted to name it after King George III of England, since the king helped pay for Herschel's work. The name that Herschel suggested was Georgium Sidus, which means "George's Star" in Latin. Many people didn't like the name because it linked the discovery to the monarch, who was not very popular at the time. Also, many felt the name was too long and wordy.

Other name suggestions poured in. Someone actually suggested that it be named Dumbbell because astronomers the world over were kicking themselves for not having discovered the planet earlier. A more serious suggestion was Herschel, after its discoverer. French astronomy maps referred to the planet as Herschel for a number of decades.

Johann Elert Bode, the editor of a German astronomy journal, suggested the name Uranus. This name followed the established pattern of naming the planets after mythological figures. In ancient mythology, Uranus, the first sky god, was the father of Saturn. Saturn, in turn, was the father of Jupiter, and Jupiter was the father of Mars. The name Uranus was distinctive, and it created a welcome new addition to the previously established family of mythological names. By 1847, Uranus was officially recognized as the name of the newly discovered planet.

The KAO Flight

For years after the discovery, astronomers continued to observe Uranus. Advancements in telescopes and mathematics allowed scientists to make better predictions of Uranus's orbit. Stargazers became accustomed to viewing the blue-green dot. Recording its movements, along with those of the other planets, turned into business as usual until yet another discovery would turn all eyes again toward Uranus.

In 1977, an American team of astronomers boarded a converted military jet named the *Kuiper Airborne Observatory* (*KAO*). The jet carried a 36-inch (91 cm) telescope and other equipment designed to study Earth's atmosphere. On March 10, the astronomers pointed the telescope toward a star that would soon be parallel to Uranus's orbital path. They expected Uranus to block the light of the star, similar to an eclipse.

Instead of a shadow, they saw a flicker, like a light flashing on and off. They then observed another flicker and yet another. Over a short period of time, they counted at least five flickers before the edge of Uranus had even crossed the star's path. Something was traveling in front of the star, but what could it have been?

At the end of Uranus's orbit past the star, the flickers occurred again. An astronomer aboard the plane joked that Uranus must have rings like Saturn, but his colleagues dismissed the idea. Rings are bands of material that may consist of things like rocks, dust, and ice, which are attracted by the pull of a planet's gravity. As their name suggests, rings create unbroken circles or ovals around certain planets.

When the *KAO* landed, data gathered from the flight revealed that the ring theory was no joke. Just as waving your hand quickly in front of a light creates the illusion of flashing, the rings of Uranus produced the same effect on the star. What had begun as a relatively routine expedition had resulted in the first discovery of a planetary ring system in 350 years. Less than a decade later, the *Voyager 2* spacecraft would reveal further surprises about Uranus.

Two

The Planet's Unique Qualities

Until the late twentieth century, most information about Uranus came from guesses and telescope viewings. Astronomers wanted to get near the planet for closer study. A big year for Uranus was 1977, not only because of the *KAO* flight, but also because in that year all four of the Jovian planets would be aligned in such a way that one spacecraft could travel by each one. Such an alignment only occurs once every 175 years.

Space scientists had to act quickly or else lose this opportunity during their lifetimes. Astronomers planned what they called the Grand Tour of the planets with the spacecraft *Voyager 2* to be launched into deep space.

Voyager 2 approached Uranus in January 1986, nine years after it was launched. The spacecraft was still 59,000 miles (95,000 kilometers) away from the planet, but that was a lot closer than telescopes on Earth, which were a distant 1.75 billion miles (2.8 billion km) away. This was so far that the data sent back from *Voyager 2* took almost three hours to reach Earth traveling at the speed of light. The information allowed scientists to make a list of probable specifications for Uranus. Information gained from the *Voyager 2* mission, along with new scientific research, has added to our knowledge about the planet.

A November 2002 proposal by scientists at the University of Zurich in Switzerland suggests that Uranus and the other planets

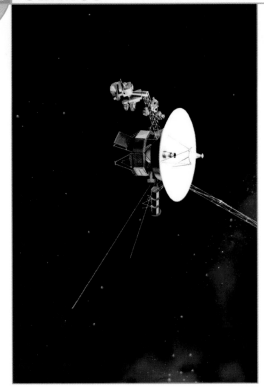

Voyager 2 has made some of the most stunning discoveries about Uranus to date. An illustration of the spacecraft on its way to Uranus is shown here.

in our solar system formed from a spinning cloud of dust, gas, and ice called a protoplanetary disk. This formation occurred approximately 4.5 billion years ago, when all of the planets formed from the same basic materials.

A Mass of Gas

Before *Voyager 2*, scientists speculated that Uranus consisted of several layers of gas and a vast ocean. A new theory supports the idea that the planet has only a few basic layers: a rocky core, a thin crust with icelike substances, and a superdense gassy atmosphere. This atmosphere is composed of

Voyager 2, A Fully Loaded Spacecraft

The *Voyager 2* spacecraft looks like a giant satellite dish with a few ladderlike arms sticking out. Every part of the craft serves an important function. The round disk at its center is equipped with a strong antenna. The base of the disk mostly contains fuel and mechanical components. Television equipment and cameras rest at the end of one arm, while a magnetism meter sits at the end of another arm. A long radio antenna juts out from the back of the craft. While no human passengers are aboard *Voyager 2*, this loaded flying robot has provided invaluable information about planets at the outer edges of our solar system.

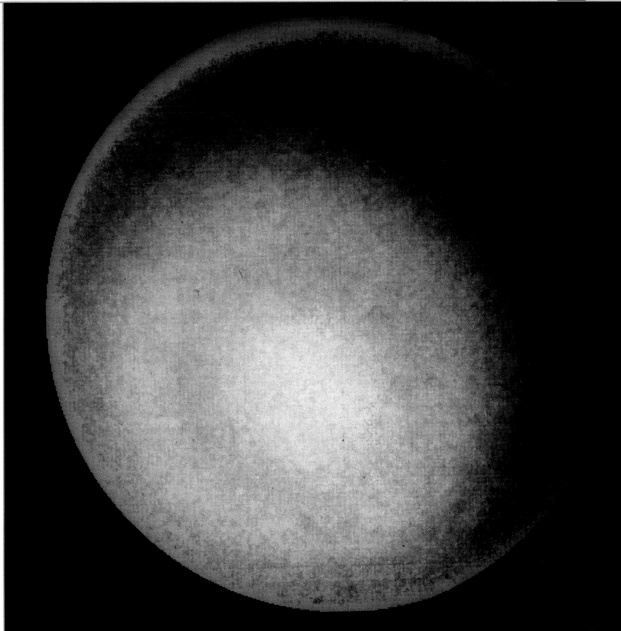

This computer-enhanced image of Uranus taken by *Voyager 2* shows the haze in the planet's upper atmosphere. Clouds, however, are obscuring much of the upper atmosphere. In addition to the distance Uranus is from Earth, these obstructions make the planet a particularly difficult one to study.

approximately 83 percent hydrogen, 15 percent helium, and 2 percent methane. These gases have no taste, odor, or color. Methane also absorbs red waves of light coming from the Sun. The absence of red is what gives Uranus its blue-green color.

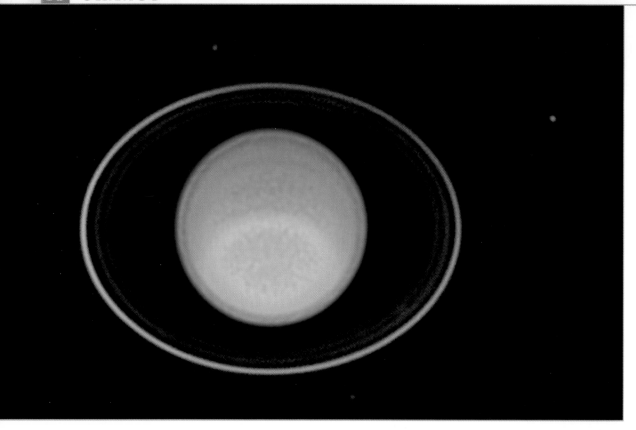

Surprisingly, the Hubble Space Telescope, which orbits Earth, has taken more detailed photos of Uranus than *Voyager 2*, which flew by the planet. The reason why Hubble's photos are so much more informative is that they were taken with a lens that detects infrared light. The infrared images allowed astronomers to tell what the atmosphere was made of. The different colors in this photo represent the different chemicals in the atmosphere.

Gas is much lighter than solids and liquids, such as rock and water. Imagine a balloon filled with helium versus a balloon filled with water. A water balloon has weight and can drop to the ground. But a helium-filled balloon can float into the air because helium is lighter than air.

Because Uranus is composed of lightweight gases, the planet has one quarter of Earth's density even though it is 14.5 times heavier than Earth. (Density is a measurement of the amount of mass within a certain amount of space.) Since mass and density affect gravity, the force that holds us to the ground, the strength of gravity on Uranus is 90 percent of that found on Earth's surface. If you weighed 150 pounds (68 kilograms) on Earth, you would weigh only 135 pounds (61 kg) on Uranus.

The Planet's Sideways Tilt

One of the most unusual features of Uranus is that the planet lies on its side. Uranus looks like it was knocked over by a heavyweight boxing champion, which in this case could have been a celestial object the size of Earth that crashed into Uranus not long after its formation.

Earth and most of the other planets spin around like a top. Uranus spins around similar to a ball rolling down a hill because it tilts 98 degrees away from its axis, the imaginary line through the center of a planet. Earth has a tilt too, but it is around 23.5 degrees. That is why most globe models show Earth tilted slightly to one side.

The Uranus Calendar

A day is equal to one rotation on a planet's axis, or one spin. For example, it takes Earth twenty-four hours to complete one full spin. This is why one day on Earth is equal to twenty-four hours. Uranus has a shorter day. It takes only seventeen hours and fourteen minutes for it to rotate on its axis.

A year is equal to the time it takes for a planet to orbit, or revolve around, the Sun. Earth travels for 365.26 days before completing its journey. This is why one year on Earth is equal to approximately 365 days. Because Uranus is 1.78 billion miles (2.8 billion km) away from the Sun, the trip takes much longer than it does for Earth, which is 93 million miles (150 million km) from the

Shown here are the rings of Uranus taken by the *Voyager 2* spacecraft. To get a sense of the size of the rings, the top frame of this image, from edge to edge, is approximately 6,214 miles (10,000 km) across. The streaks in the background are stars. The exposure of this photo was 96 seconds, which is why the stars are shown as streaks.

Sun. A year on Uranus lasts an incredible 30,685 Earth days. That means a year on Uranus equals about 84 Earth years!

A Magnetic Mystery

The device that measured magnetism onboard *Voyager 2* detected that Uranus possesses a very strong magnetic field, a region where electrical forces exist and can be measured. Earth also has such a field. In Earth's core, very hot metals, such as iron and nickel, are believed to produce its magnetic field. This field is what causes compass needles to move, giving us a sense of direction. It is like having a giant magnet at the center of our planet.

On Uranus, the axis of the magnetic field is tilted 59 degrees from the planet's rotation axis. The tilt leads some researchers to suspect that the source of Uranus's magnetism may lie outside its core. Based on mathematical modeling, a number of scientists now believe that the magnetic field of Uranus is generated in its thin crust. Fluid movement in electrically charged regions within the crust could be creating the planet's magnetism.

Rings Galore

The rings first detected during the *KAO* flight proved to be just a handful of rings in Uranus's impressive ring system. *Voyager 2* revealed that the planet has at least eleven rings ranging in size from 1 mile (1.5 km) wide to 60 miles (96 km) wide.

While scientists are not yet certain what these rings are made of, most speculate that the rings consist of large pieces of ice covered with a substance that astronomers speculate contains carbon. Astronomers think carbon is present in the ice chunks because the rings are dark in appearance. Many substances on Earth, such as charcoal and coal, are made out of carbon, too.

Three

An Unusual Landscape

The composition of Uranus, while not yet fully understood, is unusual by Earth's standards. It's not, however, completely unusual for the rest of our solar system. Just as the name Uranus fits into the family of planetary names, so too does the makeup of the planet itself.

Some scientists even think of Uranus as the Sun's colder twin. Like Uranus, the Sun is a ball of gas. The Sun at its formation was much larger than the planets. It had enough pressure to generate the nuclear and chemical reactions that resulted in the big ball of fiery gas we now see and feel from the sky. The difference between Uranus and the Sun, though, is that we can feel the heat the Sun generates, while Uranus produces very little heat.

An Ocean or All Atmosphere?

Shortly after the *Voyager 2* data was received, researchers speculated that Uranus must consist of three layers. The first layer in this model is the planet's rocky core. The middle layer is a tremendous ocean containing water under high pressure. The pressure could be high enough to create an electrical charge within the water. The charged water could gain even more electrical force as the planet rotates on its axis. The electric ocean theory provided one explanation for the magnetism measured by *Voyager 2*. The third and outer layer is the gassy atmosphere.

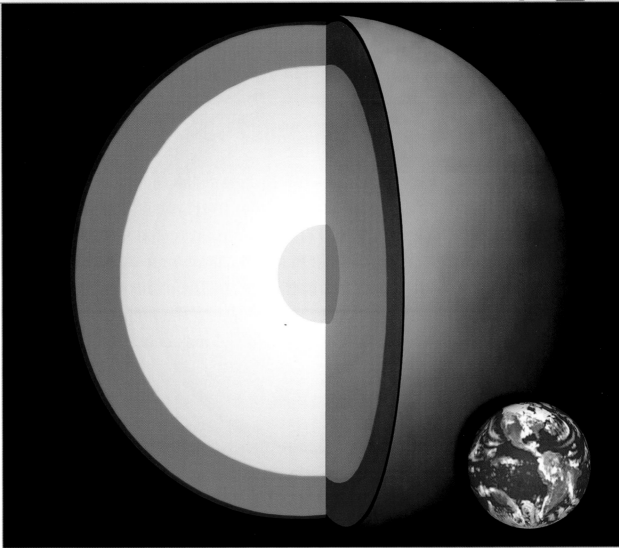

Shown here is a computer-generated diagram of Uranus's composition. At the center (gray) is a dense rocky core. Outside of this core (white) is a layer of water ice and other ices. Outside of that is a layer of liquid hydrogen, which eventually gives way to a gaseous atmosphere. At the bottom right is a model of Earth to compare both planets' relative sizes.

A problem with this model is that a planet composed primarily of water should bulge out in the middle near the equator. Imagine a water balloon. If you were to spin the balloon around, the force of the spin would cause more liquid to collect at the middle of the balloon, creating a slight bulge. But Uranus has no such bulge around its equator. Most astronomers now suspect that Uranus consists of a rocky core; a layer with a fluid, icelike mixture made of ammonia, hydrogen sulphide, methane, and water; and a gaseous atmosphere.

A Planet Made of Diamonds?

Surprises may yet lie underneath Uranus's superdense atmosphere. Some scientists think the pressure that likely exists on Uranus and the planet's rocky core could create the right recipe for diamond formation. If so, it is possible that trillions of large diamonds are located below the atmosphere. It might be the challenge of future explorers to figure out how to travel through the atmosphere to see exactly what treasures the blue-green veil may conceal.

Many Moons

Moons are celestial bodies that revolve around planets. Earth has one moon. Uranus has at least twenty-seven. Stargazers may find

Uranus by the Numbers

- Diameter: 31,764 miles (51,119 km)
- Age: About 4.5 billion years old
- Length of Day: 17 hours and 14 minutes
- Average Rotation Speed: 4.2 miles per second (6.8 km/s)
- Revolution Period: 84 Earth years
- Average Temperature: -350° Fahrenheit (-212° Celsius)
- Mass: 86,849,000,000,000,000,000,000,000 kilograms
- Number of Rings: 11
- Number of Moons: 27 discovered to date
- Trips to Uranus: 1

even more Uranus moons in the future, since telescope technologies continue to improve. In fact, three moons of Uranus, each about the size of San Francisco, were discovered as recently as September 2003.

Before the *Voyager 2* mission, Uranus was thought to have only five moons: Titania and Oberon, both discovered in 1787; Ariel and Umbriel, found in 1851; and Miranda, documented in 1948. *Voyager 2* revealed ten more: Puck, Cordelia, Ophelia, Bianca, Cressida, Desdemona, Juliet, Portia, Rosalind, and Belinda. Most of the moons were named after characters in plays by William Shakespeare.

In the 1990s, another series of moons was discovered. Stargazers identified Caliban and Sycorax in 1997. In 1999, astronomers saw Stephano, Prospero, and Setebos for the first time. From 2001 to 2003, researchers spotted seven other moons. Researchers say more Uranus moons must exist. Observations of the rings around the planet provide clues about the moons. Similar to how our moon's gravitational pull affects tides on Earth, the rings on Uranus get their oval shape from the nearby moons. The rings wobble slightly and possess thin, sharp edges. Numerous moons could be pulling the rings into this defined shape.

The Five Biggest Moons of Uranus

Ariel, Miranda, Oberon, Titania, and Umbriel are the largest moons orbiting Uranus. Tonight, take a closer look at our moon. If it is a clear night, you should not have any trouble seeing it in the sky. It is impressively big when compared with most moons in our solar system, including those of Uranus.

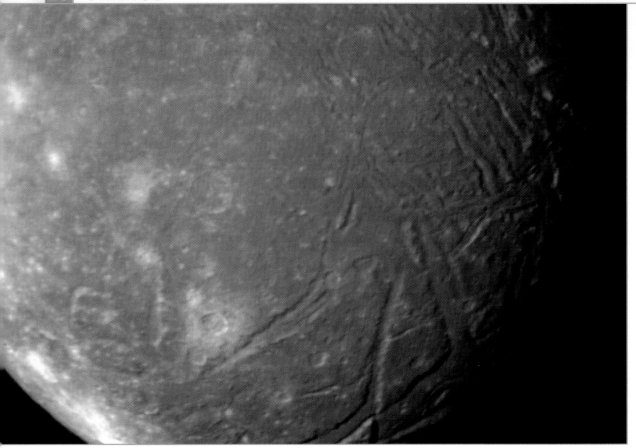

Ariel, a Uranian moon, is shown here in a color image taken by *Voyager 2* from a distance of 105,000 miles (170,000 km). The complex terrain of craters, fault scarps (or low steep slopes), and valleys is visible.

All five of Uranus's largest moons are much smaller than Earth's moon. Despite the size and distance from Earth of the Uranus moons, the *Voyager 2* expedition and telescope images have provided us with photographs and detailed information about them. Uranus's moons possess unique features. Many experts think they are the strangest celestial bodies in the universe.

Ariel

Ariel is the brightest of the Uranus moons. Most stars, moons, and satellites shine because of a combination of two processes: light reflection and energy released from the center of the celestial bodies.

This energy travels to the surface, where it is radiated into space as light, which observers can see from Earth. Since Ariel's surface appears to be relatively inactive, its brightness is probably due to light reflecting off of ice on the surface of Ariel. Sheets of ice, along with craters, give Ariel a scarred surface. Most moons show scarring, usually caused by collisions with other moons, planets, comets, meteors, or other objects in space.

Oberon

Oberon has even deeper craters than Ariel, some as deep as 12 miles (19.3 km). That is almost twice the height of Mount Everest, the tallest mountain on Earth.

Even more unusual is the presence of a mysterious black substance at the bottom of many of Oberon's craters. Researchers have no idea what the black substance is. It likely resulted from volcanic activity and then hardened on Oberon's surface.

Titania

Titania is the largest moon of Uranus. One of its valleys, the Messina Chasma, extends for 900 miles (1,448 km), which is about three times the size of the Grand Canyon here on Earth. Impacts on Titania probably caused water and ice to seep to the surface of the moon. When water freezes it expands, which could have caused some of Titania's cracks, valleys, and craters.

Umbriel

Umbriel is the darkest Uranus moon, save for one striking feature: a very bright ring shape. This ring shape is visible on the moon's surface. Nicknamed "the fluorescent Cheerio" after the breakfast cereal, this distinctive ring is likely ice at the bottom of a crater.

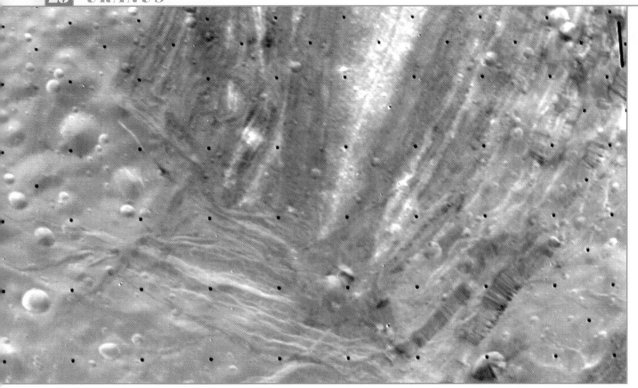

Uranus's moon Miranda has one of the most interesting surfaces of all the planet's moons. This image of Miranda was taken by *Voyager 2* from a distance of 19,263 miles (31,000 km). Visible are the fractures, craters, and grooves. The complex surface suggests that the moon had a geologically eventful past.

The rest of Umbriel is dark, probably due to the presence of carbon, which may be mixed with rock and ice on this moon.

Miranda

If a prize existed for the universe's weirdest moon, Miranda surely would be a contender. On most moons and planets, patterns exist on the surface. Miranda, on the other hand, is a jumble of craters, cracks, and incredibly steep cliffs. One cliff leads into a 12-mile (20 km) deep canyon. There is also a big "V" shape on the surface, and a series of mysterious ovals 200 miles (322 km) across. The entire moon looks like a mismatched mess. Some experts speculate that Miranda formed from a bunch of satellites that collided and stuck together like a giant popcorn ball.

Four

A Hostile Climate

Seeing something from a distance makes it hard to see its interesting features. For example, a television showing an exciting movie could capture your attention if you are nearby. When viewed from very far away, the television may just look like a boring box with nothing changing on its screen.

For years, researchers thought nothing changed on Uranus. But in the past several decades, scientists have seen that Uranus is a dynamic place with plenty of action and changes occurring every day. Sometimes these events, like seasonal changes, are hard to study because Uranus is so different from Earth. The unusual tilting rotation of the planet creates incredibly long seasons that would be impossible for humans to tolerate.

The next time winter gets you down and has you longing for summer, remember that seasons on Uranus last for approximately twenty years. The lengthy seasons are due to the planet's tilt and distance from the Sun.

The Unbearable Cold

Temperatures everywhere on Uranus measure at approximately -350°F (-212°C). The frigid conditions occur both day and night, and seem to last throughout the year with little variation. The planet's constant chill is likely due to the weak sunlight and the composition of Uranus. The sunlight that does reach Uranus seems to distribute evenly around the planet. Strong winds also help to spread out the Sun's dim rays.

The Whipping Wind

Air and gases in our atmosphere undergo continual movement and circulation. In our jet stream, which is a fast-moving current of air in Earth's upper atmosphere, winds move at approximately 100 miles per hour (161 km/h). Winds in the upper atmosphere of Uranus whip around at 200 miles per hour (322 km/h), twice as strong as what we experience here on Earth.

The direction of the winds on Uranus also surprised the scientists studying *Voyager 2* data. On Earth, prevailing winds blow in a west-east direction because our planet rotates from west to east. Because sunlight hits the poles of Uranus directly, experts thought that winds on the planet would travel from north to south. Instead, the major winds on Uranus blow from east to west. The planet's tilt and speedy rotation overpower the Sun's influence on wind direction.

The Bright Clouds

In keeping with the earlier image of Uranus as a boring planet, astronomers could not detect any clouds around it. For quite a while, it was thought that Uranus had no clouds at all. But recently, the National Aeronautics and Space Administration's (NASA) Hubble Space Telescope found twenty distinct clouds. They appear to be orange in color, probably due to the reflection of sunlight mixed with the planet's blue-green hue. They are some of

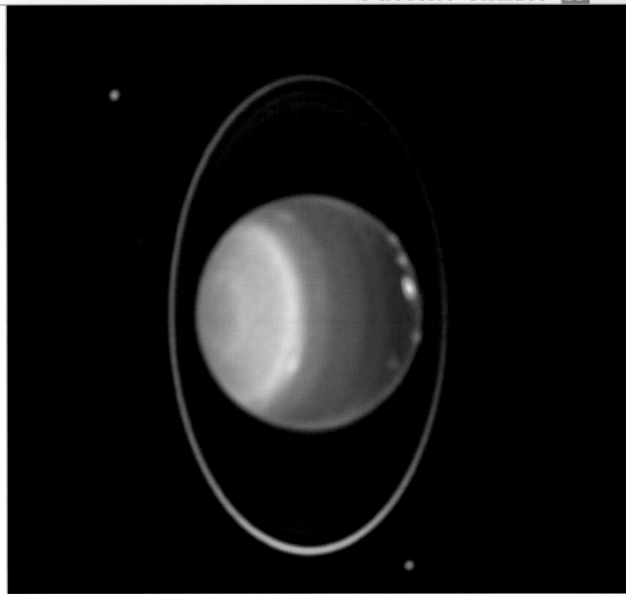

This color-enhanced image of Uranus and its rings was taken by the Hubble Space Telescope. The bright spots to the right of the planet are newly discovered clouds. There are about twenty in total.

the brightest clouds in the universe. Perhaps this is because of frozen material creating a twinkle effect.

Most of Earth's clouds look as though they are fluffy objects that move slowly. This is not the case on Uranus. Clouds there zip around the planet at more than 300 miles per hour (483 km/h).

Spring Storms

In 1999, the Hubble Space Telescope captured springtime on Uranus. The time-lapse movie revealed massive storms covering a distance of about 1,250 miles (2,011 km), or about the distance from New York to Kansas. During spring, Uranus experiences one such storm after another. Temperatures still hover around -300°F (-184°C).

The film provides a rare view of Uranus coming out of its twenty-year winter. When sunlight moves past the poles, it warms the atmosphere around the planet. This appears to stir the hydrogen, helium, and methane gases, which leads to storms. Similar seasonal activity occurs on Earth, though with not nearly as much intensity. That is because Earth tilts only slightly on its axis.

Rainbows and Color

The orange, blue, and green colors of Uranus are the product of light waves. Light is a form of energy that travels in waves. Sunlight has a mixture of different wavelengths. A rainbow appears when light passes through water, a prism, or another kind of medium that can bend light waves. Rainbows show many colors produced by sunlight. Moving from long to short waves, the colors red, orange, yellow, green, blue, and violet make up rainbows.

Since it probably does not rain on Uranus, it is doubtful that the planet has any rainbows. Methane gas, however, absorbs long color wavelengths, like red. Without the reddish hues from sunlight, the planet always has a blue-green color.

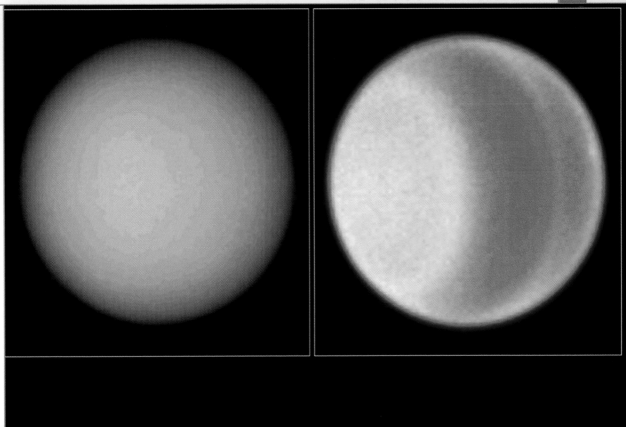

These images of Uranus were taken by the Hubble Space Telescope on July 31 and August 1, 1997. Clouds are beginning to appear on the planet, which indicates the arrival of spring. The aqua image on the left has been color enhanced to show what the planet would look like to the human eye. The red image on the right shows methane molecules in the atmosphere.

Lightning

As if speeding clouds, whipping winds, and terrible storms were not enough, Uranus also seems to have tremendous bolts of lightning. *Voyager 2* recorded static interference similar to what we can hear when listening to a radio during an electrical storm.

Astronomers believe the lightning on Uranus is much more powerful than what we get on Earth. Turbulence in Uranus's atmosphere generates static electricity. This electricity can then explode into giant sparks of lightning.

Five

The Future Possibilities

Though scientists have gathered a lot of information about the planet's size, composition, rotation, orbit, and climate, a number of questions about Uranus remain unanswered. Does life exist on the planet? Will there be another expedition to Uranus? What will the future hold? These are just a few unsolved mysteries surrounding the blue-green planet. Educated guesswork can provide some possible answers.

Life Unlikely

Humans, animals, birds, plants, and all other living creatures on Earth that we know of probably could not live in the inhospitable conditions of Uranus. Even so, scientists have not ruled out the possibility that life exists on other planets, even ones with hostile environments like Uranus.

One reason is that researchers are still finding creatures that can survive in extreme environments on our own planet. Hydrothermal vents on Earth's sea floor release mineral-rich water that measures over 752°F (400°C). Microbes live in and around these vents and feed off the minerals. Conversely, microbes in glaciers can withstand extremely cold temperatures well below the freezing point. We have not even found all forms of life on Earth, much less begun to fully explore possible life in space.

Uranus is so far away from the Sun that temperatures on the planet are extremely cold. Even if the planet has water, which is required for life as we know it, scientists feel that no life could survive the extreme temperatures. One possibility for life, however, is hydrothermal vents, such as these found on the floor of the Pacific Ocean. Vents like these release heat from the planet's interior and allow life to thrive in cold environments.

The Next Mission

Uranus is on a long waiting list of planets that astronomers would like to explore further. Since the planet exists at the outer edges of the solar system, where life is not as likely to be found as it is on Mars and the moons of Jupiter, Uranus must take a backseat for now. *Voyager 2* could be the closest we will get to the planet in our lifetime.

It is possible that a visit to Uranus could be linked with an expedition to another planet, as it was for the Grand Tour in the 1970s and 1980s. Scientists have already speculated that any kind of permanent observation of Uranus would have to take place on one of its moons, since there is no land on the planet itself. In the distant future, a tiny, unmanned space station might be set up on Miranda to get a better look at Uranus.

In addition to finding more moons, it is possible that more rings and clouds will be found near the planet. Since rings primarily consist of celestial debris, such as rocks, the ring matter can be the size of a paper clip or as big as a house. Rings made from smaller debris near Uranus may be spotted in the future, as observation techniques on Earth improve.

Currently, astronomers rely upon the Hubble Space Telescope and other powerful ground-based telescopes to study Uranus. NASA's Terrestrial Finder program is working on a telescope called a coronagraph with an extremely large mirror that could indicate oxygen, water, ozone, air, and other substances on planets. More clouds will likely be documented in the years to come as

Extraterrestrial Life

When searching for extraterrestrial life, astronomers mainly focus on Mars, along with Europa, Titan, and Io, three moons of the planet Jupiter. One thing that is necessary for life as we know it is water. While the air on Mars, Europa, and Io would be toxic for humans and animals, water may once have flowed on these celestial bodies. Water may still even be present underneath their surfaces, especially that of Europa. The moon Europa is quite cold, but if nutrients and gases are trapped under its icy surface, life could thrive as it does in icebergs, glaciers, snowbanks, and other extremely cold, icy places on Earth.

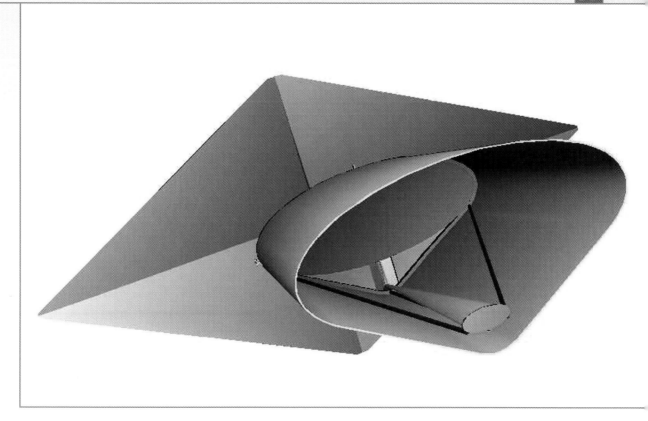

Shown here is a computer-generated prototype for the visible light coronagraph. This large telescope, with a mirror three to four times bigger and ten times more precise than that of the Hubble, will be able to collect even the faintest light from distant stars. It will also be able to block out light from nearby stars, thus reducing glare.

seasons change on Uranus. Space experts are focusing on the year 2007, when Uranus will experience its next summer.

Clues for Another Planet?

In the two centuries following the discovery of Uranus, astronomers found the planets Neptune and Pluto. Uranus led stargazers to believe that these two planets existed because of irregularities observed in the orbit of Uranus. All celestial bodies exert a gravitational pull on each other, so the scientists investigated what was doing the pulling.

Slight wobbles and inexplicable movements by Uranus, Neptune, and Pluto suggest that there could be a tenth planet in our solar system influencing their orbits. Irregularities in the movement of these planets sometimes exist between the calculations conducted at major observatories, such as the U.S. Naval Observatory, the Royal Observatory in Greenwich, England, and the Paris Observatory in France. Pluto was only first documented in 1930. Space experts hesitated to eliminate the possibility that a tenth planet could be located during the new millennium. Outside of our solar system, future discoveries are a certainty. In March 2004, NASA announced the discovery of the "planetoid" Sedna, which orbits beyond Pluto.

Watch for Yourself

William Herschel made his own telescope, as did Clyde Tombaugh, the stargazer who discovered Pluto. Today, it is easy to buy telescopes. You can also visit your local planetarium and use the telescope there. Some people claim to view Uranus without any kind of magnifying device, like binoculars or a telescope, but perfect vision and substantial knowledge of the stars and planets would be necessary to see the planet with your eyes alone. For most people, it helps to use a telescope.

To find Uranus, first look for Mars. Mars usually looks like a reddish orange dot in the sky. Although Uranus is over a billion miles away from Mars, it appears close to Mars in the sky from our viewpoint. With a telescope, look for a tiny disk of blue-green in the constellation Aquarius. If you have trouble finding the planet, check the space map that usually comes with commercial telescopes or consult with the experts at your local observatory.

Remember that great astronomers like Copernicus, Galileo, and Herschel once were curious students and stargazers. With persistence and luck, maybe one day you will find a new moon or ring of Uranus, or even a new planet.

1690: The first known reference to Uranus is made by Englishman John Flamsteed, but he did not know that it was a planet and did not get credit for its discovery.

1787: Uranus's moons Titania and Oberon are discovered.

1851: Uranus's moons Ariel and Umbriel are discovered.

1977: In August, *Voyager 2* is launched. It is scheduled to explore Uranus. It eventually discovers the moons Puck, Cordelia, Ophelia, Bianca, Cressida, Desdemona, Juliet, Portia, Rosalind, and Belinda.

The military jet *KAO* is launched, carrying a telescope designed to study Uranus.

1999: The Hubble Space Telescope views springtime on Uranus.

Uranus's moons Stephano, Prospero, and Setebos are discovered.

2007: Scientists may focus on a new mission when Uranus will experience its next summer.

1781: German-born musician William Herschel spots Uranus in March and is eventually credited with its discovery.

1847: Uranus is officially recognized as the name of the newly discovered planet.

1948: Uranus's moon Miranda is discovered.

1986: *Voyager 2* approaches Uranus in January.

1997: Uranus's moons Caliban and Sycorax are discovered.

2001–2003: Researchers discover seven moons of Uranus.

2002: In November, a new proposal by scientists at the University of Zurich suggests that Uranus and the planets in our solar system formed from a spinning cloud of dust, gas, and ice called a protoplanetary disk approximately 4.5 billion years ago.

Glossary

astronomy The study of space and the objects in space.

astronomer A person who studies space and the objects in space.

atmosphere The collection of gases surrounding a celestial body.

axis An imaginary straight line running through the center of a planet.

celestial Of or relating to space.

climate The weather patterns of a particular region of a planet.

density A measure of the matter within a specific amount of space.

gravity The pull that celestial bodies have on each other and material objects.

Jovian planets The planets that are related to, or are similar to, Jupiter. In addition to Jupiter, the Jovian planets are Uranus, Saturn, and Neptune. They all consist mainly of gas and are also known as the gas giants.

magnetic force The properties and power of attraction generated by a magnetic field.

orbit A path in space along which a celestial body, such as a planet, moves.

planet Any one of the nine discovered massive bodies revolving around the Sun.

protoplanetary disk The spinning cloud of dust, gas, and ice from which all planets likely formed around 4.5 billion years ago.

satellite Any object that orbits around a planet, such as a moon.

solar system A term used to describe the Sun and all of the planets that orbit around it.

theory An idea or assumption that is not proven.

universe Space and all celestial bodies that exist in it.

For More Information

Exploratorium
Science Information Infrastructure
3601 Lyon Street
San Francisco, CA 94123
(415) 397-5673
Web site: http://www.exploratorium.edu/learning_studio/sii

Kennedy Space Center
Spaceport U.S.A.
Kennedy Space Center, FL 32899-0001
(321) 452-2121
Web site: http://www-pao.ksc.nasa.gov/kscpao/visit/visitor.htm

National Aeronautics and Space Administration (NASA)
300 E Street SW
Washington, DC 20546
e-mail: comments@hq.nasa.gov
Web site: http://www.nasa.gov

Smithsonian National Air and Space Museum
Seventh Street and Independence Avenue SW
Washington, DC 20560
(202) 357-2700
Web site: http://www.nasm.si.edu

Space Telescope Science Institute
Johns Hopkins University
Homewood Campus
3700 San Martin Drive
Baltimore, MD 21218
(410) 338-4700
Web site: http://oposite.stsci.edu

Web Sites

Due to the changing nature of Internet links, the Rosen Publishing
Group, Inc., has developed an online list of Web sites related to the
subject of this book. This site is updated regularly. Please use this
link to access the list:

http://www.rosenlinks.com/lnp/uran

For Further Reading

George, Linda. *Uranus.* Farmington Hills, MI: Gale Group, 2002.

Goss, Tim. *Uranus, Neptune and Pluto.* Portsmouth, NH: Heinemann Library, 2002.

Kerrod, Robin. *Uranus, Neptune and Pluto.* Minneapolis: Lerner Publishing Group, 2003.

Rau, Dana Meachen. *Uranus.* Minneapolis: Compass Point Books, 2002.

Shepherd, Donna Walsh. *Uranus.* New York: Franklin Watts, 2004.

Stefoff, Rebecca. *Uranus.* New York: Benchmark Investigative Group, 2002.

Stewart, Melissa. *Uranus.* New York: Scholastic Library Publishing, 2001.

Stille, Darlene R. *Uranus.* Chanhassen, MN: The Child's World, Inc., 2003.

Tocci, Salvatore. *A Look at Uranus.* New York: Franklin Watts Library Edition, 2003.

Bibliography

Asimov, Isaac. *Uranus: The Sideways Planet*. Milwaukee, WI: Gareth Stevens Publishing, 1988.

Branley, Franklyn M. *Uranus: The Seventh Planet*. New York: Thomas Y. Crowell, 1988.

Brimner, Larry Dane. *Uranus*. Danbury, CT: Children's Press, 1999.

Davis, Don, and Donald K. Yeomans. *The Distant Planets*. New York: Facts on File, 1989.

Fradin, Dennis B. *Uranus*. Chicago: Children's Press, 1989.

Jackson, Francine. *The Outer Planets*. Danbury, CT: Grolier Educational, 1998.

Kerrod, Robin. *Uranus, Neptune, and Pluto*. Minneapolis: Lerner Publishing Group, 2003.

Litmann, Mark. *Planets Beyond: Discovering the Outer Solar System*. New York: Wiley Science Editions, 1988.

Ridpath, Ian. *The Illustrated Encyclopedia of Astronomy and Space*. New York: Thomas Y. Crowell Publishers, 1979.

Vogt, Gregory L. *Uranus*. Brookfield, CT: The Millbrook Press, 1993.

Index

About the Author

Jennifer Viegas is a reporter for Discovery News and is a features columnist for Knight Ridder Newspapers. She has worked as a journalist for ABC News, PBS, the *Washington Post*, the *Christian Science Monitor*, and several other publications.

Credits

Cover, pp. 4–5, 16, 26, 37 NASA/JPL/CalTech; pp. 8, 11 © Science Photo Library/Photo Researchers, Inc.; p. 12 © Bettmann/Corbis; p. 17 NASA/U.S. Geological Survey; p. 18 NASA/Erich Karkoschka/ University of Arizona Lunar and Planetary Lab; pp. 20, 28 NASA NSSDC; p. 23 © Mark Garlick/Science Photo Library/Photo Researchers, Inc.; p. 31 NASA/Kenneth Seidelmann, U.S. Naval Observatory; p. 33 NASA/Heidi Hammnel/Massachusetts Institute of Technology; p. 35 © Peter Ryan/Scripps/Science Photo Library.

Designer: Thomas Forget; Editor: Nicholas Croce